Visual ⊕ Explorers

Space

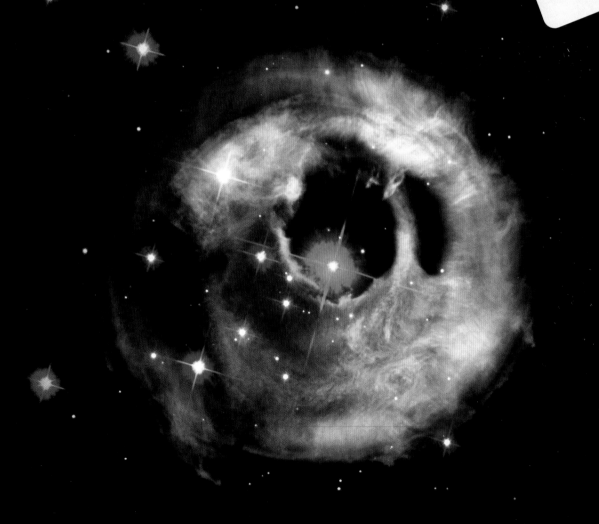

BARRON'S

All inquiries should be addressed to:
Barron's Educational Series, Inc.
250 Wireless Boulevard
Hauppauge, NY 11788
www.barronseduc.com

ISBN: 978-1-4380-0829-5
Library of Congress Control Number: 2015956074

Date of manufacture: January 2016
Manufactured by: Toppan Leefung Printing Co, Ltd., China

9 8 7 6 5 4 3 2 1

Image credits: (t) top, (m) middle, (b) bottom, (r) right, (l) left, (FF) Fact file.
Flickr – p11 (main, t) David Hopkins; FF (3rd) Olga Stavrakis. **p21** (b) Neil Zeller. **p27** FF (1st) RV1864, (3rd) Dan Beaumont Space Museum. **p29** FF (1st) Michael Layefsky, (2nd) C.E. Worthington, (3rd) RCSUN36.

Getty Images – p26 (bl) Keystone-France Picture.

NASA and ESA – FC: (main) NASA; (l-r) NASA/ESA/M. Livio and the Hubble 20th Anniversary Team (STScI); NASA/JPL-Caltech; NASA/GSFC/SDO; NASA. **BC** (l-r) NASA Cassini-Huygens Mission 2006/2007; NASA/JPL-Caltech/MSSS; NASA/ESA/Hubble Heritage Team/STScI/AURA/R. Gendler/J. GaBany; NASA Johnson. Spine: NASA/JPL/Space Science Institute. **p1** NASA/ESA/H.E. Bond (STScI). **p4** (ISS) NASA. **p6** (main) NASA/SDO; (bl) NASA/SDO/Amari. **p7** (t) NASA Goddard, (m, Sun) NASA/SDO, (m, craft) NASA/SOHO, (b) NASA. **p8** (main, r) NASA/JPL; (main, l) NASA/Johns Hopkins University Applied Physics Laboratory/ Carnegie Institution of Washington; (bl) NASA/JHU APL. **p9** (t) NASA/Johns Hopkins University Applied Physics Laboratory/Carnegie Institution of Washington; (m) NASA/JPL; (b) NASA/SDO/AIA. **p10** (main) Reto Stöckli/Nazmi El Saleous/Marit Jentoft-Nilsen/ NASA/GSFC. **p11** FF (t) NASA. **p12** (main) NASA/JPL/USGS; (bl) NASA/Don Davis. **p13** (tr) NASA/Sean Smith (mb) NASA; **p14** NASA. **p15** (tl) NASA/JPL; (tr) G. Neukum (FU Berlin) et al/DLR/ESA; (m) NASA; (b, Mars) NASA Hubble STScI/AURA; (b, Deimos, Phobos) NASA; FF NASA. **p16** (main, l) NASA/JPL/Space Science Institute; (main, r, DYK) NASA. **p17** (t) NASA/ JPL; (m, planet) NASA Cassini-Huygens Mission 2006/2007; (m, craft) NASA/JPL-Caltech; FF (t) NASA/JPL/DLR, NASA, NASA, (b) Galileo Project/DLR/JPL/NASA. **p18** (main, r) NASA. **p19** (t, m, r) NASA/JPL-Caltech, (tl) NASA/JPL; (m) NASA; (b) NASA/JPL. **p20** (main) NASA; (bl) NASA/JPL. **p21** (t) NASA/JPL-Caltech; (m) ESA/MPAe Lindau; FF (3rd–5th) NASA/JHUAPL/SwRI; NASA/ESA/A. Feild (STScI); R. Hurt (SSC-Caltech)/JPL-Caltech/NASA. **p22** (main) NASA/ESA/H. E. Bond (STScI); (bl) NASA/JPL-Caltech. **p23** (t) ESA/NASA/L. Calcada (ESO for STScI); (m) NASA/JPL-Caltech; (b) Illus Martin Kornmesser/ESA/ECF. **p24** (main, X-ray) NASA/CXC /Caltech/P.Ogle et al, (optical) NASA/STScI, (IR) NASA/JPL-Caltech, (radio) NSF/NRAO/VLA; (bl) NASA. **p25** (t) NASA/ESA/H. Teplitz and M. Rafelski (IPAC/ Caltech)/A. Koekemoer (STScI)/R. Windhorst (Arizona State University)/Z. Levay (STScI); (b) NASA; FF (t–b) NASA; ESA/Hubble & NASA-Judy Schmidt; ESA/NASA/JPL-Caltech/STScI. **p26** (main) ESA/ATG medialab. **p27** NASA; FF (m) NASA. **p28** (main) ESO/L. Calçada. **p29** (t) NASA; (m) NASA/JPL/University of Arizona. **p30** (main) NASA's Goddard Space Flight Center. **p31** (t) ESA/ATG medialab; (b) NASA Goddard's Scientific Visualization Studio. **p32** NASA/JPL/Space Science Institute.

Shutterstock – p2-3 Yuri Dmitrienko. **p4** (b/g) Matej Pavlansky, (bl) Hollygraphic. **p5** (t) MarcelClemens, (Sun) Aphelleon; (m) Kevin Key, (Earth) Ismagilov. **p10** (bl) SantiPhotoSS. **p11** (m) Kristijan Zontar; (b) simonekesh; FF (m) Anton Balazh. **p13** (tl) Paul Prescott; (FF) Tristan3D; **p18** (main, l) Mopic. **p21** FF (2nd) Marc Ward.

Other contributors: p5 (b) CERN. **p17** (b) StefanPWinc. **p18** (bl) Mike Young. **p21** FF (t) Thierry Lombard. **p28** (bl) Matthew Hunt (scotchtape.ductwhisky.com). **p29** (b) Tom Blackwell (tjblackwell.co.uk/lucid). **p30** (bl) Smithsonian National Air and Space Museum. **p31** (m) OHB System AG.

Introduction

When the Russian satellite, Sputnik 1, was launched into space in October 1957, it marked the beginning of the Space Age. Sputnik 1 spent three months orbiting Earth, gathering information that advanced knowledge of near space and spacecraft design. Many missions and technological advances later, so much more is known about the Universe, and all of it fascinating. Join the Visual Explorers mission to get up close to planets, stars, asteroids, and more.

Contents

Read on for a **journey** of **discovery** into **space**...

What is space?

The term **space** refers to what we see when we look up at the night sky. What we can see is actually the **visible** Universe. While Earth is part of the **Universe**, we tend to view space as beginning **62 miles** (100 km) above Earth's surface. The Universe is everything that exists! It is all existing matter, from the particles that build **atoms** to **enormous** galaxies. Less than five percent of it consists of normal **matter** that you can see, like planets and stars; the rest is dark energy and dark matter that can only be **detected** through witnessing its gravitational **impact** on other objects.

Facts and figures

Movement
Our solar system travels around the Milky Way at an average speed of more than 500,000 miles (800,000 km) per hour.

Solar system
A solar system is a star and the bodies that orbit around it.

Rotation
Rotation of an object is the time it takes to turn once around its axis. One Earth rotation is one Earth day.

Orbit
An orbit is the path an object takes to travel around another object. One Earth orbit of the Sun takes one year.

Solar system travel
It takes our solar system about 230 million years to rotate around the center of our galaxy, the Milky Way.

Astronomy
Astronomy is the scientific study of the physical Universe.

Did you know?

You can see more than stars in the night sky if you know where to look. You will also see planets, meteors, and constellations (groups of stars that make up recognizable patterns).

Orion, the hunter, constellation

The International Space Station (ISS) is a laboratory in a low orbit over Earth

Cosmology looks at the theory behind the nature and origins of the Universe.

Light years

Space is so big that distance has to be measured in light years, which is the distance light travels in one year. One light year is equivalent to 5.9 trillion miles (9.5 trillion km).

A big bang

The Universe began about 13.8 billion years ago in a huge cosmic explosion coined the Big Bang.

The solar system

Our solar system was formed more than 4.5 billion years ago. It consists of the Sun and everything that orbits around it. This includes planets and their moons as well as countless numbers of small objects, such as asteroids, comets, dust clouds, and meteorites, all of which are kept in orbit by the Sun's gravity.

Our solar system

Mercury Earth Jupiter Saturn

Venus Mars Uranus Neptune

Asteroid Belt **Kuiper Belt**

The Milky Way as seen from Earth

The Milky Way

Our solar system is located within the Milky Way, where it makes up a minuscule amount of the total mass. Born 13.8 billion years ago, it will likely exist for many more billions of years. It is possible to see the Milky Way stretching across a night sky if you are far away from light pollution.

Hadron Collider

The Large Hadron Collider (LHC) is a huge particle accelerator. It "throws" high-energy particles to reach the speed of light, then uses a 17-mile (27-km) ring of magnets to make them collide. The aim is to recreate conditions after the Big Bang so scientists can understand how the Universe began.

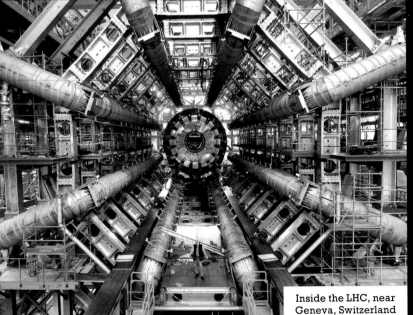
Inside the LHC, near Geneva, Switzerland

Fact file

Atmosphere

Earth is surrounded by a protective atmosphere that is made up of five principal layers. The atmosphere becomes thinner as it gets further from Earth.

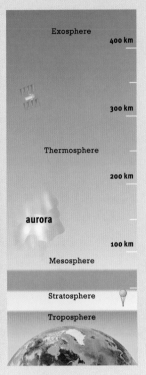

Exosphere
400 km

300 km

Thermosphere
200 km

aurora
100 km

Mesosphere

Stratosphere

Troposphere

Troposphere

The first and lowest layer of Earth's atmosphere is where weather occurs.

Stratosphere

The ozone layer, which absorbs most of the Sun's radiation, is in this region.

Mesosphere

The lowest temperatures, down to -130°F (-90°C), are found in this layer.

Thermosphere

The hottest of all of the layers, temperatures can rise above 3,632°F (2,000°C).

Exosphere

The exosphere is the outer layer, which fades into the vacuum of space.

The Sun

The Sun is the **center** of our solar system, around which everything **revolves**. The Sun, the only star in the solar system, has a diameter of almost **1 million miles** (1.4 million km), big enough for one million Earths to fit inside, and has a mass **750** times bigger than all of the planets in the solar system combined. Huge amounts of **energy** are generated by the **super-hot core** in the form of light and heat. While the Sun is not a particularly special **star** within the greater Universe, it is essential to Earth for **light** and heat. **Without** the Sun, Earth would turn to ice and life would cease.

Facts and figures

Sun's profile
Radius: 432,169 mi (695,508 km)
Surface temperature: 9,932°F (5,500°C)
Core temperature: 27 million°F (15 million°C)
Rotation time: 27 Earth days
Age: 4.5 billion years

History
Many ancient cultures throughout history have placed great importance upon the Sun. They worshipped Sun gods, like Ra and Inti, and created structures to align with the Sun's calendar.

Shape
Despite being made of gas, the Sun is close to being a perfect sphere.

The future
In a few billion years the Sun will die, eventually becoming a white dwarf star.

Nuclear fusion

Huge pressures and high temperatures at the core of the Sun cause hydrogen atoms to fuse together, converting them into helium. This process is known as nuclear fusion.

Blinding light

The Sun's rays are so strong that it must never be looked at directly as it could cause permanent damage to your eyesight.

Did you know?

Solar flares are a sudden release of built-up magnetic energy in the solar atmosphere. Though short-lasting, they can send huge amounts of energy into space.

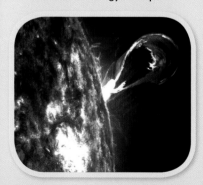

The radiation emitted by the largest X-class solar flares can reach Earth

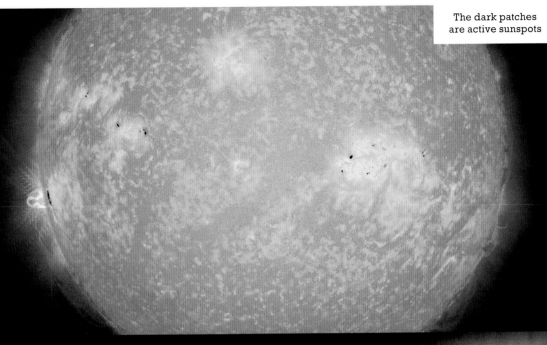

The dark patches are active sunspots

Sunspots

Sunspots are darker, cooler patches that appear on the Sun's surface. These patches are caused by disturbances within the Sun's magnetic fields. They can last for a couple of hours or several months. The largest sunspot observed – AR 2192 – was 14 times the size of Earth.

The SOHO

In 1995, the European Space Agency (ESA) and NASA launched the Solar and Heliospheric Observatory (SOHO), a satellite built to observe the Sun. The SOHO has revolutionized our knowledge of the Sun while warning us of sun storms heading toward the Earth.

An artist's impression of the SOHO gathering information

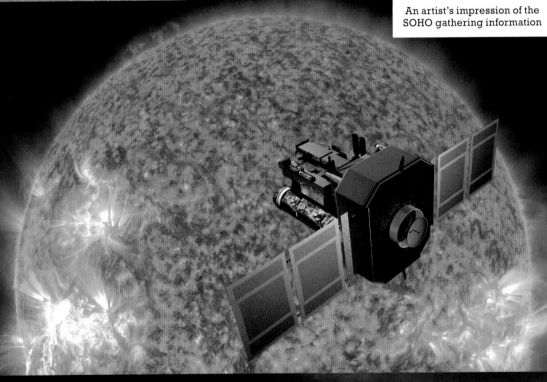

It takes about eight minutes for sunlight to reach Earth.

The surface

The surface of the Sun is called the photosphere. It is made of a layer of gas 311 miles (500 km) thick.

Mass of the Sun

The Sun makes up 99.8 percent of all the mass in our solar system. All the planets and space rock account for only 0.2 percent.

Solar eclipse

A total solar eclipse is a rare astronomical event that happens when the Moon comes directly between the Sun and the Earth. The Moon blocks the Sun from view and turns day to night on Earth. A solar eclipse is the only time when the Sun's chromosphere layer is able to be seen from Earth.

The Moon blocking out the Sun on Earth

Mercury and Venus

Mercury is the closest planet to the Sun and the first in our solar system. A **dry**, rocky planet, Mercury is covered with many wide and deep craters. While **scorching** hot during the day, temperatures can drop way below freezing during the night. **Venus** is regarded as Earth's **sister** planet, as it is most like Earth in regard to its size, composition, and cloudy **atmosphere**. With a surface temperature of up to **864°F** (462°C), Venus is a blisteringly hot, arid planet due to its proximity to the Sun and its mostly carbon dioxide **"greenhouse** gas" atmosphere trapping the heat.

Facts and figures

Mercury's profile
Distance from the Sun: 36 million miles (58 million km)
Radius: 1,516 miles (2,439.7 km)
Temperature: -279.4–+800°F (-173–+427°C)
Rotation time: 59 Earth days
Orbit time: 88 Earth days
Number of moons: 0

Venus's profile
Distance from the Sun: 67 million miles (108 million km)
Radius: 3,760 miles (6,051.8 km)
Temperature: 863.6°F (462°C)
Rotation time: 243 Earth days
Orbit time: 225 Earth days
Number of moons: 0

Mercury is the smallest planet in our solar system.

At first glance, Mercury's surface looks similar to that of Earth's Moon

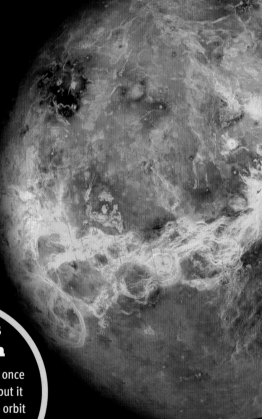

Did you know?

On August 3, 2004, NASA launched the spacecraft *Messenger* to discover more about Mercury. Very little was known at the time about the solar system's smallest planet.

Tiny planet

Mercury is a lot smaller than Earth, meaning there is less gravity. If you weigh 150 lb (68 kg) on Earth, on Mercury you would weigh about 57 lb (25.7 kg) – less than half the amount.

Venus's rotation

Venus spins on its axis once every 243 Earth days, but it takes 225 Earth days to orbit the Sun, making its year shorter than one rotation.

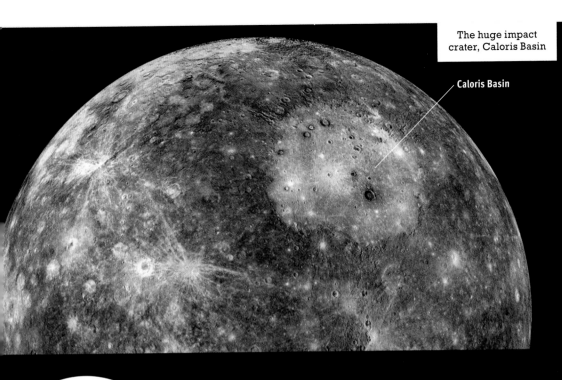

The huge impact crater, Caloris Basin

Caloris Basin

Meteor impact

Over the course of 4.5 billion years, Mercury has been hit millions of times by meteorites and asteroids. The most famous impact crater is Caloris Basin, which is approximately 960 miles (1,550 km) across. Being so large, it is filled with craters caused by subsequent asteroid collisions.

Venus's surface

Beneath the thick, acid cloud that surrounds Venus, there is a desert-like surface of flat rocks, mountains, and canyons. Venus is well-known for its enormous volcanoes, the tallest being Maat Mons, which is a staggering 5 miles (8 km) high with lava flows hundreds of miles in length.

Maat Mons, Venus's spectacular volcano

Heavy planet

Despite being only a third of the size of Earth, Mercury is almost as heavy. It is incredibly dense due to its metal core.

Hot, hot, hot

While Mercury is closest to the Sun, Venus is the hottest. Climate change on Venus caused its water to evaporate.

The few spacecraft that have landed on Venus's surface have survived no longer than two hours

The transit of Venus

Venus passes across the Sun every 105 years, generally with sightings coming in pairs of eight years. After the second sighting, it will not be seen for another century. From Earth, Venus appears to be a small, black blob moving across the Sun. Venus's next transit is due in 2117.

Composite of Venus's 2012 transit across the Sun

Earth

Geologists have determined that planet Earth is more than **4.5 billion** years old. Our planet is unique in many ways; the most significant is that the atmosphere and **climate** have created the perfect environment for life. It is the only planet known to have **water** in all three states, liquid water being the most important as it is the key to **life**. Earth also has an atmosphere, which not only provides air to **breathe**, but also acts as a **barrier** by reflecting more **harmful** forms of solar energy, like radiation.

Facts and figures

Earth's profile
Distance from the Sun: 93 million miles (149 million km)
Radius: 3,958 miles (6,371.00 km)
Temperature: -126−+136°F (-88−+58°C)
Rotation time: 24 hours
Orbit time: 365.3 days
Number of moons: 1

Deepest point
The Marianas Trench is 7 miles (11 km) below sea level.

Volcanoes
A volcano is caused by one tectonic plate sliding under another.

Hurricanes
These powerful storms have wind speeds of 157 miles (252 km) per hour.

Earthquakes
These occur when tectonic plates conflict and release energy.

Earth's past

Earth was once a ball of molten rock. As it cooled, the magma ocean solidified into Earth's crust. The mantle is still cooling down.

The seasons

Earth rotates on a tilted axis, creating the seasons. The polar regions have only two seasons: summer, when the sun does not set, and winter, when it does not rise.

Did you know?

Planet Earth is home to approximately 8.7 million different species of life. Three-quarters of these species live on the land, while one-quarter live in the vast waters of the planet.

Earth has an exceptionally diverse environment with deserts, both hot and cold, glaciers, mountain ranges, and rainforests

Our atmosphere consists of **78** percent **nitrogen** and **21** percent **oxygen** plus **trace gases.**

The sprawling Himalayas in Asia

Ice sheets
The Antarctic and Greenland ice sheets contain more than 99 percent of the fresh water on planet Earth.

Tectonic plates

The Earth's crust consists of large plates. These plates move between 1–6 in (3–15 cm) a year in a process known as continental drift. Over time, if two plates collide and push the crust up, the result is a mountain range. Tectonic plates are also responsible for earthquakes and volcanoes.

Inside Earth

Earth consists of four main layers: the inner core, the outer core, the mantle, and the crust. The inner core is made of iron and nickel and is the hottest part of Earth. The outer core is also made of iron and nickel, but it is molten. The mantle is semi-molten rock, while the crust is solid rock.

Inner core Outer core Mantle Crust

A cross section of Earth's four layers

Oceans
The largest body of water on Earth is the Pacific Ocean, taking up a third of Earth's surface. It's also the deepest ocean.

Magnetic field

Earth has a very strong magnetic field caused by the spinning of the metal in the outer core. Despite its strength, it does have weak spots through which high-energy particles from space can enter, causing auroras. We know these colorful lightshows as the northern (Borealis) and southern (Australis) lights.

A spectacular aurora lightshow over Earth

Rivers
The Amazon, Earth's widest river—25 miles (40 km) in wet season—is also one of the longest—4,000 miles (6,400 km).

The Moon

The Earth has only one natural **satellite** – the Moon. It is, on average, **239,000 miles** (384,400 km) from Earth, making it close enough to detect some of the **features** on its surface with the naked eye. With a telescope, you can see the Moon's **mountains**, plains, and valleys. The Earth and Moon have been **together** for approximately 4.5 billion years. There have been **121** missions to the Moon; however, only nine of them were **manned** spacecraft. Due to its lack of **water**, the Moon cannot support life. Though a lot **smaller** than Earth, it influences our planet in many ways.

Did you know?

Scientists believe the Moon was created when an object collided with Earth, throwing out chunks of Earth's crust into space. The debris bound together to create the Moon.

As the Moon has little atmosphere, there is nothing to protect it from incoming comets

The dark side

It takes the same amount of time for the Moon to orbit Earth as it does to spin on its axis, meaning we only see one face of the Moon.

Light as a feather

The Moon's gravity isn't as strong as Earth's, which makes walking normally impossible. It requires astronauts to hop or glide over the Moon's cratered surface.

The **face of the Moon** we **don't see** is **known** as the **"dark side of the Moon."**

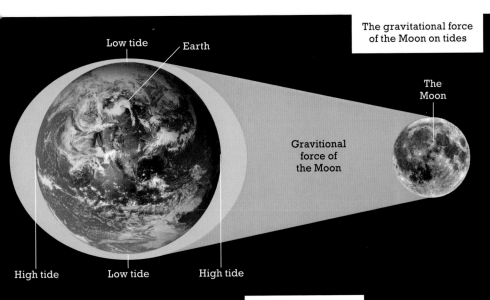

Low tide · Earth

High tide · Low tide · High tide

The Moon

Gravitional force of the Moon

Earth's tides

Although much smaller than Earth, the Moon's gravity has the power to control Earth's tides. As the Moon orbits Earth, its gravitational effect pulls water toward it, creating low and high tide bulges. The points on Earth closest and farthest from the Moon have high tide simultaneously.

Fact file

Moon phases

The Moon goes through eight key phases during its orbit around the Earth. Known as the lunar month, it takes 29.5 days to complete these phases.

New Moon (Moon not visible)

Waxing crescent

First quarter or "half Moon"

Waxing gibbous

Full (face illuminated)

Waning gibbous

Third quarter or "half Moon"

Waning crescent

The surface

The surface of the Moon is covered in rock and a fine gray dust. The Moon has mountains, plains, and valleys and, as a result of meteor collisions, many craters, ranging greatly in size from a few inches to hundreds of miles.

Moon landing

On July 16, 1969, history was made when a human was finally able to travel to the surface of the Moon. As part of NASA's *Apollo 11* mission, four days after launch, astronauts stepped foot on the Moon for the first time. Since then, there have been five more successful Moon missions, with a total of 12 people having walked on the surface.

The many craters on the Moon's surface

James B. Irwin – 8th astronaut on the Moon

Mars

Mars is the fourth planet from the Sun. It is frequently referred to as the **Red Planet** and more is known about Mars than any other planet in the solar system. Mars is named after the **Roman** god of war because of its blood-red **color**. Its red appearance is caused by the atmosphere on the planet turning the **iron** in the soil to **rust**. Mars's atmosphere is 95 percent carbon dioxide, making it **unsuitable** for human life. If humans were to **live** on Mars they would need to withstand winds that can create dust clouds **620 miles (1,000 km)** above the planet's surface.

Facts and figures

Mars's profile
Distance from the Sun: 142 million miles (228 million km)
Radius: 2,106 miles (3,389.5 km)
Temperature: -243–+68°F (-153–+20°C)
Rotation time: 24.6 Earth hours
Orbit time: 687 Earth days
Number of moons: 2

Mars's seasons
Like Earth, Mars also has four seasons.

Valles Marineris
The Valles Marineris is a system of canyons that run along the equator of Mars.

Missions
Of the 43 missions to Mars, only 20 have been successful.

Visible from Earth
Mars is one of the brightest, most visible objects in our night sky.

Humans in space

The unmanned *Rover* mission in 2020 will investigate how human exploration of Mars might be carried out. *Rover* will gather rock samples for eventual study back on Earth.

Water found

In September 2015, scientists confirmed there is water – most probably salty – on Mars. The search is now on to learn the source of the water.

Did you know?

Mars's surface resembles that of a desert. It is covered in a thick layer of red Martian dust that, in places, has piled up in small sand dunes. Mars's dust is as fine as talcum powder.

Mars's surface is rocky, with many canyons, volcanoes, and craters

Mars has ice caps on both poles

Olympus Mons

Mars is home to Olympus Mons, which is the largest volcano on Mars and the largest known volcano in our solar system. It is 388 miles (624 km) in diameter and 15.5 miles (25 km) high, making it three times the height of Mount Everest. It is believed that Mars's volcanoes stopped erupting when the planet's core began to cool.

Olympus Mons, the largest known volcano

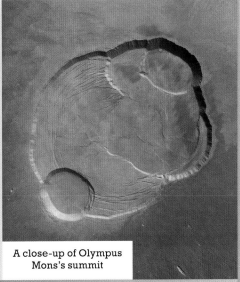

A close-up of Olympus Mons's summit

Curiosity "selfie" on the Red Planet

Support life?

In 2011, as part of NASA's Mars Science Laboratory (MSL), the *Curiosity Rover* was sent to Mars to see if the planet could support small lifeforms called microbes. A camera mounted at the end of the rover's robotic arm took the first ever Mars "selfie" in August 2015. It marked a full Martian year (687 Earth days) spent on the planet.

Mars's moons

Mars has two moons – Phobos and Deimos. Due to their small size and irregular shape, it is believed they were once asteroids caught in Mars's gravitational pull. Both moons are heavily cratered, with Phobos having a particularly large impact crater.

Deimos

Phobos

Mars with its two orbiting moons

Fact file

Mars missions

There have been many missions to Mars – not all successful. Those that have been successful have provided a wealth of scientific information.

Viking 1

Viking 1 was the first spacecraft to successfully reach the surface in 1976. It transmitted the first photos of Mars's surface.

Mars Climate Orbiter

Due to human error in calculating the force of its thrusters, the Orbiter burned up as it hit Mars's atmosphere in 1999.

The *MAVEN*

The *Mars Atmosphere and Volatile Evolution Mission* (*MAVEN*) space probe was launched in 2013 to study Mars's upper atmosphere.

Jupiter and Saturn

Lying beyond the **Asteroid Belt** is Jupiter, the first of the gas giants. **Jupiter** is the largest planet in the solar system, with more than **twice** the mass of all the other planets in the solar system combined. Jupiter's **atmosphere** is mainly hydrogen and helium gases, like the Sun's. **Saturn** is the second largest planet in the solar system and another **gas** giant. Saturn is known for its **series** of seven spectacular rings. Made mostly of gas, Jupiter and Saturn do not have a **solid** surface like the planets closer to the Sun. It would be **impossible** to stand on these planets!

Facts and figures

Jupiter's profile
Distance from the Sun: 483 million miles (778 million km)
Radius: 43,441 miles (69,911 km)
Temperature: -198–+8.6°F (-128–-13°C)
Rotation time: 10 Earth hours
Orbit time: 12 Earth years
Number of moons: 62-67 known moons

Saturn's profile
Distance from the Sun: 870 million miles (1.4 billion km)
Radius: 36,183 miles (58,232 km)
Temperature: -288°F (-178°C)
Rotation time: 10.2 Earth hours
Orbit time: 29 Earth years
Number of moons: 62

It would take 317 Earths to equal the mass of Jupiter, a giant planet

Saturn's rings have a diameter of 175,000 miles (282,000 km) and some sections are only 32 ft (10 m) thick

Jupiter's rings

NASA's *Voyager 1* discovered Jupiter's ring system in 1979. Jupiter's Gossamer rings are made of small particles of dust.

Did you know?

In 2011, NASA launched the *Juno* spacecraft to Jupiter. It is expected to reach the planet in 2016 and its task is to gather information on Jupiter's formation, atmosphere, and evolution.

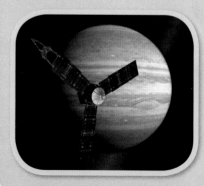

Saturn's rotation

Gas giant Saturn rotates on average once every 10.2 hours. This high rotational speed means that it significantly bulges around its equator, giving it flattened poles.

Jupiter's 10-hour rotation gives it the shortest day.

Great Red Spot winds reach speeds of 263 mph (423 km)

Jupiter's moons

Jupiter has many orbiting moons—the most recent was discovered in 2003. The four largest moons are Europa, Io, Callisto, and Ganymede.

Europa

Europa is covered in ice 62 miles (100 km) thick. It is believed that there is an ocean of water beneath the ice.

Io

Covered in hundreds of volcanoes, Io is the most volcanically-active object in our solar system.

Callisto

Callisto is a mixture of ice and rock, and is the most heavily-cratered object in our solar system.

Ganymede

Ganymede is not only Jupiter's largest moon, it is the largest moon in our solar system.

Extreme weather

Jupiter has some of the most violent weather of all the planets. The ferocious storms possibly give the planet its distinctive striped look. One of Jupiter's most famous features is the Great Red Spot, a giant atmospheric storm, akin to a hurricane. First recorded in 1664, the storm is still raging today.

The *Cassini* orbiter studying Saturn

Saturn mission

Launched in 1997, the *Cassini-Huygens* mission was an ambitious endeavor to reach Saturn. In 2004, after almost seven years travel, it reached its destination. The scientific probe, *Huygens*, was parachuted to the surface of Titan, Saturn's largest moon, while the *Cassini* orbiter began orbiting the ringed planet.

Saturn's rings

In many photos, Saturn's rings appear to be solid but they are not – it appears this way because they consist of billions of dust, rock, and ice fragments that vary in size from tiny dust particles to huge boulders, rotating at extremely high speeds.

The rocks, dust, and ice of Saturn's rings

Uranus and Neptune

Uranus is the seventh planet from the Sun and the third largest after Jupiter and Saturn. Uranus is an icy giant with a **system** of thin, faint rings that were not discovered until the late **1970s**. In 1986, *Voyager 2* was able to **transmit** images showing there were **13 rings**. Uranus is the only planet in the solar system to rotate on its side, doing so every 17 hours. Like Uranus, **Neptune** is an **icy** giant that also has a system of rings. At a distance of 15 billion miles (4.5 billion km) from the Sun, Neptune receives very **little** light or heat. Neptune appears blue because of the **methane** gas in its atmosphere.

Moons of Uranus

Uranus has 27 known moons, the majority named after characters from Shakespeare plays. There are five major moons: Ariel, Miranda, Titania, Oberon, and Umbriel.

Side spinner

Planet Uranus is unique in that it spins on its side. Scientists believe that this was caused by a collision early in its history.

Did you know?

Uranus was the first planet to be discovered with the use of a telescope. This is a replica of the telescope used by William Herschel in 1781 when he initially saw Uranus.

Uranus has 21-year-long seasons due to its highly tilted angle

Uranus is named for the Greek god of the heavens and sky.

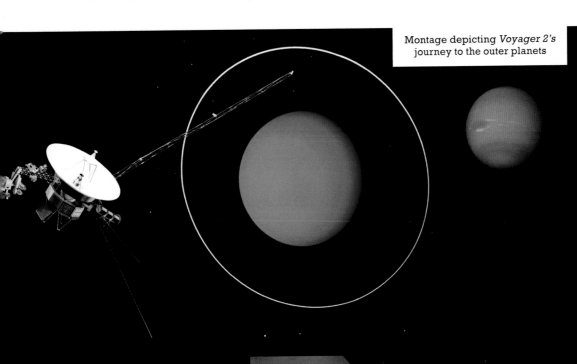

Montage depicting *Voyager 2's* journey to the outer planets

12-year journey

It took *Voyager 2* almost nine and a half years to reach Uranus. It took an additional two and a half years to get to Neptune. Most of what we know about Neptune and Uranus has come from the *Voyager 2* mission. It discovered two more of Uranus's rings and 10 more moons.

The icy moon

Neptune's largest moon, Triton, was discovered 17 days after Neptune. With a surface temperature of -391°F (-235°C), it is one of the coldest objects in our solar system. This moon is very geologically active, with its liquid nitrogen geysers erupting 5 miles (8 km) above the surface.

Triton's extremely cold, icy surface

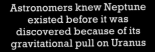

Astronomers knew Neptune existed before it was discovered because of its gravitational pull on Uranus

Blue planet

Neptune is named after the Roman god of the sea because of its vibrant blue color.

Long orbit

Since its discovery in 1846, Neptune has completed only one full orbit of the Sun. It takes 165 years for Neptune to go around the Sun.

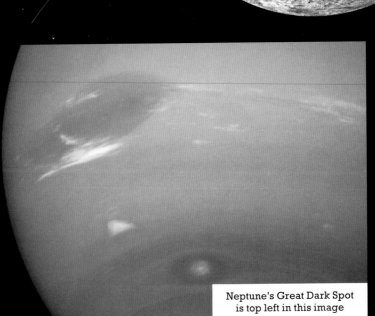

Neptune's weather

Neptune has the most extreme weather of all the planets. Winds can be up to three times stronger than Jupiter's and nine times stronger than winds on Earth. The Great Dark Spot was a storm the size of Earth, generating wind speeds of 1,305 mph (2,100 km). First noted in 1989, it had passed by 1994.

Neptune's Great Dark Spot is top left in this image

Asteroids, comets, and meteors

There aren't just planets and moons in **space**. There are plenty more fascinating objects to be found, both man-made and **natural**. There are billions of pieces of space **rock** – some huge, but **most** pebble-sized – traveling in the solar system. A lot of them are remnants left over from the formation of the **planets**. Most of our solar system's asteroids can be found in the **Asteroid Belt** or the **Kuiper Belt**. Meteoroids tend to be small pieces of **debris** that have broken off comets or asteroids. Once a **meteoroid** hits Earth's atmosphere, it becomes a meteorite.

Facts and figures

Meteor showers

The Perseids
The Perseids feature fast-moving and bright meteors that leave a trail. Their peak period of activity is in mid-August, and they appear near the Perseus constellation.

The Orionids
The Orionids meteor shower happens late October, appearing near the Orion constellation. They are formed of Halley's Comet debris.

The Leonids
The Leonids can be seen mid-November. They appear near the Leo constellation.

The Lyrids
The Lyrids meteor shower occurs mid-April, appearing near the Lyra constellation.

The Geminids
Up to 120 meteors per hour are possible at the mid-December peak. They appear near the Gemini constellation.

Image of the 2012 Lyrids meteor shower taken from the ISS

Largest meteorite

Earth's largest meteorite is the Hoba in Namibia, Africa. It landed 80,000 years ago and weighs 66 tons (60,000 kg).

The Kuiper Belt

The Kuiper Belt sits beyond the orbit of Neptune. It is made up of remnants left over from the formation of our solar system.

More than **100 tons** of **dust** and **small particles** enter **Earth's atmosphere** every day.

Did you know?

In 2004, NASA's *Stardust* spacecraft managed to collect dust samples from the tail of Comet Wild 2, helping scientists discover more about the composition of comets in space.

An artist's depiction of an asteroid family being created

Asteroids

Asteroids are lumps of rock and metal that orbit the Sun. There are over 200 asteroids in the Asteroid Belt that are more than 62 miles (100 km) in diameter. Some asteroids travel around together in "families." These families are created by asteroid collisions.

Comets

A comet consists of ice, frozen gas, dust, and pieces of rock. Its tail is a trail of gas and dust created by the comet starting to melt as it gets closer to the Sun. One of the most famous comets is Halley's Comet, which appears every 75–76 years. The earliest recorded sighting of this comet was in 446 BCE; its next visit will be in 2061.

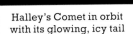

Halley's Comet in orbit with its glowing, icy tail

Meteor showers

When meteoroids hit Earth's atmosphere they burn up, causing streaks of light known as meteors, or shooting stars. While this happens all the time, there are certain times of the year when meteor showers are more common. They are named after the constellations that they appear to be coming from.

A 2014 Geminids meteor shower and Aurora Borealis

Stars

A star is a ball of **gas** that produces heat and light. Consisting mainly of hydrogen and helium, a star is held **together** by its own gravity. Stars are born out of a **nebula**, a cloud of dust and gas. Within a nebula, **gravity** compacts the gases and dust into a clump of matter. As the **clumps** get bigger they begin to break down, forming a **core** in a process called gravitational collapse. Over millions of years, the **mass** gets hotter as it is compacted. Once the temperature reaches 10 million kelvins, **nuclear** fusion begins. This keeps the star **shining** for billions of years.

Kelvin temperature

The temperature of a star is usually measured in kelvins (K). This unit was named after an Irish physicist. A kelvin is the Celsius temperature plus 273.16.

Neutron star

When large stars collapse, they throw off their remains around the cosmos. The only thing left will be a neutron star or a black hole.

Did you know?

There are an estimated 200 billion stars in the Milky Way galaxy alone. It is thought that there are at least seven new stars created every year within the galaxy.

In 2002, the V838 star expanded and, for a moment, was the Milky Way's brightest star

Artist's concept of the Fomalhaut star being orbited by its exoplanet

Exoplanets

Scientists are now able to confirm that there are stars outside of our own galaxy that have planets orbiting them. These planets are known as exoplanets. The first was discovered in 1992, and since then hundreds more have been documented.

Death of a star

When small stars die, they swell into red giants and cast off their outer layers, forming planetary nebulas. Eventually they cool and fade away, leaving behind a white dwarf star. When bigger stars become red supergiants and run out of nuclear fuel, the core collapses. This causes an explosion, also called a supernova.

A dying star shedding its layers

Orange-red **stars** are the **coolest** type of star in the **Universe.**

Star patterns

There are 88 patterns (constellations) found in the stars. Your birthday month has a constellation.

Already gone

It can take millions of years for a star's light to reach Earth. By the time we see a star, it could be that it no longer exists.

Black holes

After a star dies, a black hole may remain in its place. A black hole has a gravity that not even light can escape, which is why we cannot see it. Black holes vary in size – some being no bigger than an atom. The largest type are supermassive black holes, which tend to be found at the center of a galaxy.

An artist's representation of the black hole, Cygnus X-1

Galaxies

A **galaxy** is a system of billions of stars, nebulae, dust particles, and gas, held together by **gravity** and separated by interstellar space. There are over **100 billion** galaxies in the Universe, all of different colors, shapes, and **sizes**. The first of the galaxies are believed to have been **created** less than one billion years after the **Big Bang**, when the Universe was born. Between 2003 and 2012, NASA's Galaxy Evolution Explorer (**GALEX**), studied 10 billion years of **cosmic** history to help scientists better understand the **evolution** of galaxies, such as our Milky Way.

Facts and figures

How big?
The diameter of the observable Universe is estimated to be over 90 billion light years, although nobody knows exactly how large it is.

The brightest
The brightest known galaxy to date is WISE J224607.57-052635.0. It has the light of 300 trillion Suns.

Stars
There are an estimated 1,000 billion billion stars in the Universe.

Closest galaxy
Andromeda is the closest spiral galaxy to the Earth. It is 2.5 million light years away.

Farthest away
The most distant known galaxy, EGS-zs8-1, is more than 13 billion light years away.

Tiny galaxy
The M60-UCD1, a dwarf galaxy, contains 140 million stars densely packed together.

Did you know?

Galaxies can be found in clusters. These clusters can have a few or thousands of galaxies bound together by gravity. The Milky Way is one of 54 galaxies in the Local Group.

A rare galactic fireworks display occurring in galaxy NGC 4258

Galaxies merging

One theory on how galaxies expand is that they merge with nearby smaller galaxies in a process known as galactic cannibalism.

Better telescopes

There are an estimated 170 billion galaxies in the observable Universe. This number of detected galaxies is expected to rise with improved telescope technology.

Interstellar space is the **gas, dust, and cosmic rays** that **exist** between **stars.**

Deep Fields

The Hubble Space Telescope has taken a series of images known as the Hubble Deep Fields. For the first time, scientists have been given the ability to see formations of different types of galaxy. The first Deep Field image was taken in December 1995, showing almost 3,000 galaxies.

Galaxy nebulas

Nebulas are collections of dust and gas, and come in all shapes and sizes – some being hundreds of light years across. The Carina Nebula is an example of a reflection nebula – it reflects light from nearby stars. Dark nebula, like Horsehead Nebula, are clouds of very dense dust that block out all light.

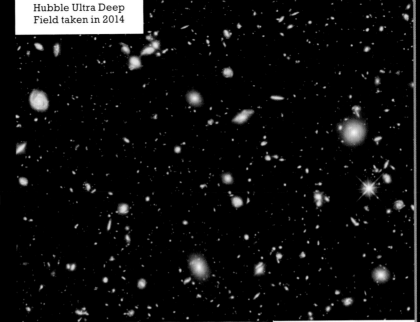

Hubble Ultra Deep Field taken in 2014

Mystic Mountain region within the Carina Nebula

Our neighbor

The Andromeda galaxy belongs to the Local Group. It is far larger than the Milky Way and it contains over one trillion stars. The Milky Way and Andromeda, both of which contain satellite galaxies, are expected to collide in about four billion years, which will create a massive spiral or disc galaxy.

Andromeda, our closest spiral galaxy neighbor

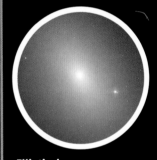
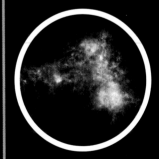

Space missions

It wasn't until the **1950s** that unmanned spacecraft, or space probes, were launched to **explore** and discover more of our solar system. Since then, many countries have launched either **manned** or **unmanned** spacecraft into space, with some of the first astronauts being **animals**. Initially, space probes were sent to look at the **Moon** and the two closest planets to Earth – Mars and Venus. Since these first **missions**, scientists have been able to send spacecraft to **discover** more about the planets in our solar system, as well as the **greater** Universe and beyond.

Did you know?

The first rocket to fly high enough to reach space was the German V-2 missile in 1942. It did not, however, manage to get high enough to stay in orbit around the Earth.

A velocity of 25,000 miles (40,000 km) per hour is needed for a rocket to escape Earth's pull.

A Soyuz rocket launches the first satellite for Europe's Copernicus environmental monitoring program

Space payloads

Between 1981 and 2011, 135 space missions were flown by space shuttles *Columbia*, *Challenger*, *Discovery*, *Atlantis*, and *Endeavour*, taking over 350 people into space.

Rocket parts

Rockets are often made of different stages, or sections. The fuel in each stage propels the rocket a little higher and then detaches.

The iconic ISS orbiting Earth in 2011

The orbiting ISS

The largest space station is the International Space Station (ISS). It travels at 17,000 miles (28,000 km) per hour with an Earth orbit time of 90 minutes. The ISS has been occupied since November 2000 and has had more than 200 people visit. The ISS is powered by solar panels that would more than cover a football field.

Space shuttle *Endeavour's* final trip into orbit in 2011

Space shuttles

NASA launched the space shuttle program, a partially reusable space vehicle that could be used to take goods into space, in the early 1980s. The shuttles were used to launch satellites and undertake scientific experiments. They also delivered sections of the ISS into space.

Life in space

Life for astronauts and cosmonauts in space is very different from life on Earth. Simple tasks, such as eating and bathing, can be challenging and require a different way of thinking. Long term, the lack of gravity can affect the bodies' strength of muscles, as well as bone density.

Astronaut Kjell Lindgren receives fresh fruit onboard the ISS

Space exploration

Since Hans Lippershey invented the first **telescope** in 1608, **technology** has grown tremendously. Lippershey's achievement of three times **magnification** is dwarfed in comparison to the magnification of the **Hubble** and other giant telescopes now used to study the **depths** of the Universe. Almost everything we know about our solar system and the world **beyond** has been **discovered** with the use of a telescope. As time and technology have progressed, telescopes have become **bigger** and far more powerful, with many now being launched into **space**.

Facts and figures

Famous space observatories

Chandra
NASA's Chandra, launched in 1999, is an X-ray observatory. It seeks out X-rays in the Universe's hot spots.

Fermi Gamma-ray Space Telescope
The Fermi Gamma-ray Space Telescope was launched into orbit in 2008. Its aim is to unveil the mysteries of supermassive black holes and more.

Spitzer Space Telescope
Launched by NASA in 2003, the Spitzer Space Telescope detects heat (infrared) radiation from new planets, exoplanets, and failed stars.

Keplar Mission
Launched by NASA in 2009, this telescope is hunting for Earth-like planets among a target group of 100,000 stars. It is looking for planets with a temperature that allows water to exist.

Did you know?

Completed in 1948, the Hale Telescope, USA, was groundbreaking for its time. Despite new telescopes having surpassed the Hale in both size and power, it is still in use.

An artist's depiction of the European Extremely Large Telescope (E-ELT) to be built in Chile, South America

The area of E-ELT's light-collecting mirror is equal to two basketball courts.

Space viewing

Space observatories make it easier to view the Universe, as Earth's atmosphere can make it difficult to obtain sharp images.

Seeing beyond

Telescopes are used to study galaxies that are too far away for spacecraft to reach. It would take a modern-day spacecraft thousands of years to reach even the closest star.

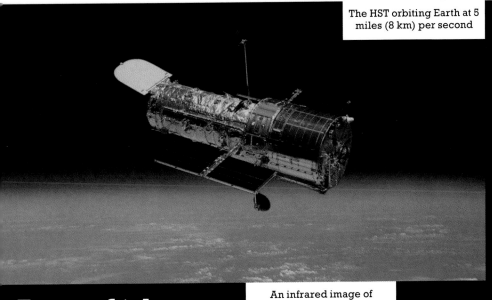
The HST orbiting Earth at 5 miles (8 km) per second

The Hubble

The Hubble Space Telescope (HST) is the world's most famous space telescope. Sent into orbit in 1990, the HST has helped scientists confirm the existence of dark energy, the age of the Universe, and much more. It has made more than 1.2 million observations since its launch.

Fact file

Earth telescopes

Observatories are home to large telescopes, many of which are at high altitudes to stay above the clouds and away from nearby light interference.

The Gemini Observatory

With one located in Chile and the other in Hawaii, the Gemini telescopes can see almost every part of the night sky.

W. M. Keck Observatory

This observatory consists of two optical and infrared telescopes on the 13,000-ft (4,000-m) high summit of Mauna Kea, Hawaii, USA.

Large Binocular Telescope

The Large Binocular Telescope, Arizona, USA, is an optical telescope with two 26-ft (8.4-m) mirrors used for collecting light.

Types of telescope

Telescopes are extremely powerful tools, detecting not just light that the human eye can see, but also radio waves, infrared light, ultraviolet radiation, and gamma rays. Each of these detect different wavelengths of energy, and have provided scientists with information about the weight, temperature, and density of atmosphere.

An infrared image of Saturn taken over 13 hours

Telescopic arrays

Radio telescopes need lots of power so instead of one enormous telescope, arrays are used. The Very Large Array (VLA) in New Mexico, USA, consists of 27 82-ft (25-m) radio telescopes arranged in a Y formation. VLA is used by scientists worldwide.

The Very Large Array discovered ice on Mercury

Satellites

A satellite is an **artificial** or natural body that orbits a planet. There are many **types** of artificial satellite and each has different **functions** – from monitoring the weather, communications, television transmission, and **navigation**. Many satellites are used to provide highly detailed images of the **Earth**. There are **three** types of satellite orbit, determined by their distance from Earth: high and **geosynchronous** Earth orbit, which is above 22,200 miles (35,780 km); **mid** Earth orbit, between 1,243–22,000 miles (2,000–35,780 km); and the most common, low Earth orbit, between **112–1,243 miles** (180–2,000 km).

Satellites are built to be as light and as strong as possible.

Facts and figures

Satellite size
Satellites come in all shapes and sizes – the smallest being no larger than the size of a football and the biggest, the ISS, being more than 300 ft (100 m) end-to-end.

Satellite launch
Satellites are usually launched into space on rockets. Once the satellite is above Earth's atmosphere, the rocket breaks away and burns up.

The oldest satellite
The oldest artificial satellite currently orbiting Earth is Vanguard 1, which was launched in 1958.

Geosynchronous orbit
Geosynchronous orbit is where a satellite matches Earth's speed, enabling it to study one particular area.

Powering satellites
Most satellites produce their own power using solar panel arrays.

Artist's concept of the Landsat 8 satellite observing Earth from an elevation of 438 miles (705 km)

Who's watching?

Some satellites in orbit are capable of seeing objects on the surface of the Earth that are three feet (one m) wide.

Space collisions

The more satellites put into orbit around the Earth, the greater the chance they will collide. In 2009, the first collision between two artificial space satellites occurred.

Did you know?

In 1957, the Soviet Union sucessfully launched the first artificial satellite, Sputnik 1, into orbit around Earth. The size of a beach ball, it only took Sputnik 98 minutes to orbit Earth.

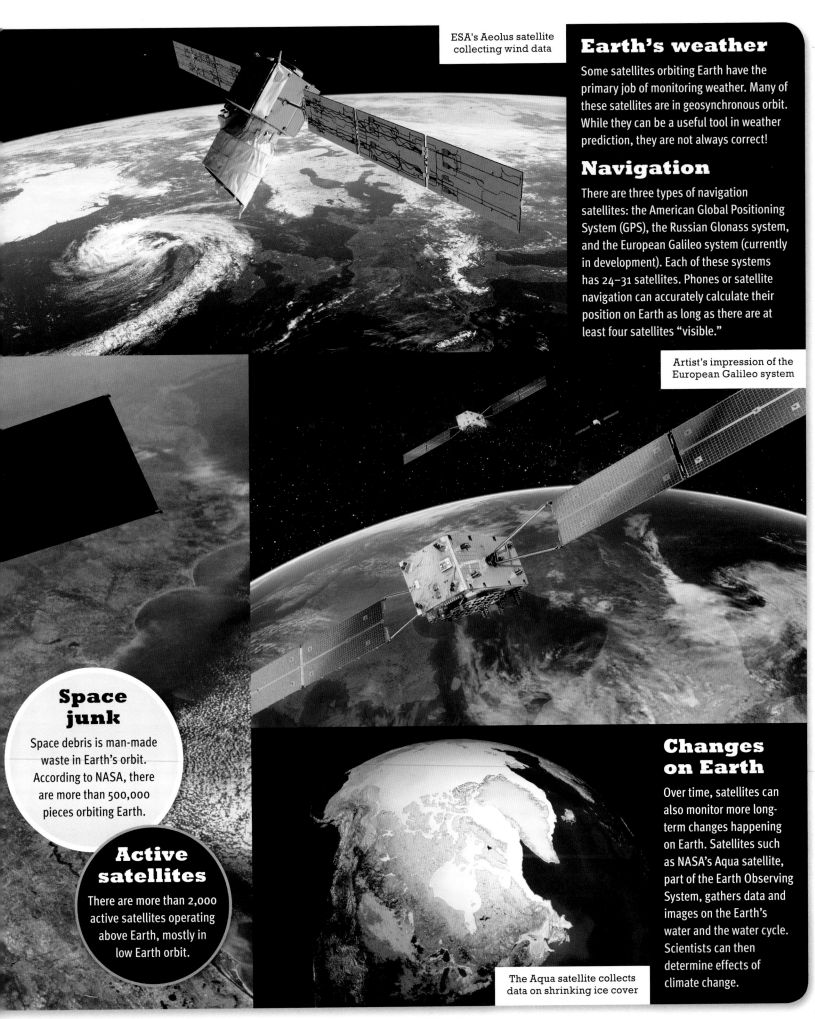

ESA's Aeolus satellite collecting wind data

Earth's weather

Some satellites orbiting Earth have the primary job of monitoring weather. Many of these satellites are in geosynchronous orbit. While they can be a useful tool in weather prediction, they are not always correct!

Navigation

There are three types of navigation satellites: the American Global Positioning System (GPS), the Russian Glonass system, and the European Galileo system (currently in development). Each of these systems has 24–31 satellites. Phones or satellite navigation can accurately calculate their position on Earth as long as there are at least four satellites "visible."

Artist's impression of the European Galileo system

Space junk

Space debris is man-made waste in Earth's orbit. According to NASA, there are more than 500,000 pieces orbiting Earth.

Active satellites

There are more than 2,000 active satellites operating above Earth, mostly in low Earth orbit.

Changes on Earth

Over time, satellites can also monitor more long-term changes happening on Earth. Satellites such as NASA's Aqua satellite, part of the Earth Observing System, gathers data and images on the Earth's water and the water cycle. Scientists can then determine effects of climate change.

The Aqua satellite collects data on shrinking ice cover

Glossary

Asteroids
These rocks of various sizes orbit the Sun. They do not have a tail.

Astronaut
Also known as a cosmonaut, this person is trained to fly a spacecraft into space.

Atmosphere
This is the envelope of gases that surrounds a planet or star.

Aurora
Light display in the sky caused by particles from the Sun activating atoms in Earth's atmosphere.

Axis
It is an imaginary line through the center of a planet or moon around which it rotates.

Big Bang
The theory that explains how everything in the Universe was formed.

Black hole
A space with super massive gravity that nothing – not even light – can escape.

Comet
A comet orbits the Sun and when close enough to the Sun has a "fuzzy" outline and tail.

Constellation
A group of stars that form a pattern or image.

Crater
Bowl-shaped hole caused by impact of a meteorite.

Dark energy
This is an unknown force that repels gravity.

Dark matter
Unseen material that is only detected because of its gravity.

Dwarf planet
An object that orbits the Sun. It has its own gravity but it is not great enough to dominate its area. There are five known dwarf planets.

Galaxy
This is a group of stars, dust, and gas held together by gravity.

Gas giant
A large planet made of gas. Jupiter, Saturn, Uranus, and Neptune are gas giants.

Gravity
A force that pulls toward the center of an object or system. Gravity causes planets to be round. Gravity can pull other objects toward a planet.

Interstellar
The space between stars.

Magnetic field
An area in which there is an electrical current or moving charged particle creating a magnetic force.

Mass
This is how much matter is in an object. It is different from weight, which is how much gravity pulls on an object.

Meteor
This is the streak of light that occurs when a meteoroid hits Earth's atmosphere. Sometimes called a shooting star. If there are many meteors, it is a meteor shower.

Meteorite
This is a meteoroid that makes it through Earth's atmosphere without burning up.

Meteoroid
This is a piece of rock or debris, often off an asteroid, that travels through space.

Moon
An object that orbits a larger planet. Some planets have more than one moon; some planets don't have any moons.

Nebula
A cloud of space dust.

Orbit
The path an object takes to circle another object.

Planet
A planet is a large object that orbits a star. Its gravity is large enough to make it dominant in its area, so many have orbiting moons. There are eight planets in the solar system.

Satellite
A natural or a man-made object that orbits another object. It is held in orbit by gravity.

Solar eclipse
When an object obscures the Sun.

Solar system
The solar system includes the Sun and all the objects – large and small – that orbit around it.

Space probe
An unmanned spacecraft that explores space and objects in space. It transmits information back to Earth.

Space telescope
A telescope that operates outside of Earth's atmosphere. It is controlled by astronomers by remote control.

Star
A glowing ball of burning gas. The Sun is the closest star to Earth.

Sunspot
A cool area on the Sun's surface that can cause solar flares or storms, which are explosive bursts of energy.

Supernova
The explosion of a star.

Universe
This consists of everything that exists: planets, stars, asteroids, space debris, black holes, and other forms of energy.

Index